The Weapon to Beat Depression
In 4 Easy Steps

Anna Kifer

The Weapon to Beat Depression: In 4 Easy Steps
© 2013 by Anna Kifer. All rights reserved. No part of this book may be reproduced in any form or by any means without permission in writing from the publisher

Blog Half Full Publishing
www.bloghalffull.com

ISBN: 978-0615836676

Preface

I am not a doctor. I am not a therapist. I am not a psychoanalyst or an astronaut or a rocket scientist. I am nothing that qualifies me to write this book EXCEPT, I was you. I wrote this book to save even just one person from the torment and pain they live with each and every day. If the hours, minutes, and seconds that I poured into this book can help even one person, then it was more than worth it.

Chapter 1

I'd like to start off by sharing a letter I received a few years ago from a former co-worker of mine. I don't recall the circumstances that lead him to contact me about his depression. However, we exchanged a couple of emails where I shared with him my struggle and how I had beaten my depression. I received this letter shortly after:

It has been about a month since I read your letter telling me a little bit about your struggles with depression and I just wanted to send you one last email to tell you what your advice and encouragement have done for me.

In your letter you talked about how pills would only mask the real problems a person was having. I have been masking my problems with pot for all of my so called 'adult life'. My normal routine was to come home from work, get high, and stay high until I went to bed. On the weekends, I would 'wake and bake', and stay high all day. I've done this for 30 years. 30 years! What a waste. I've come to believe pot, (or probably any drug a person chooses to abuse), stops a person's emotional growth, which means I don't think I've really grown emotionally at all since I was 17 or 18 years old. The night I read your email, I decided to stop using pot as a way to deaden my feelings. I gave away my weed and paraphernalia, and quit cold turkey. The withdrawal hasn't been easy, but day by day my mind feels like it's becoming clearer.

The second area where you helped is with the depression. I didn't tell you the whole truth, (probably because of embarrassment or shame), when I said I had a mild form of chronic depression. That part is true, but there have been a number of times where I've slipped into a much more serious depression. In your letter to me you said, "Our minds are a powerful thing. Trust me, mine saved my life". I could be wrong, but I think you were maybe talking about taking your own life. If I am wrong, sorry for even thinking that, but if I wasn't, I understand what you were feeling, I've been there myself. Over the years, I have thought about suicide to finally end the almost indescribable pain, despair and hopelessness that comes with deep depression. Part of my personality is to be completely self sufficient, never having to rely on other people for anything. Therefore, I've never developed any kind of support system to turn to in rough times. In the past I would just grit my teeth and hold on until it would eventually pass, but as I've gotten older, that has become harder to do. During this last episode, my life seemed to be completely unraveling before my eyes, and I had decided that I finally had enough. Not to sound too melodramatic, but my plans were pretty much set, and my bags were packed (so to speak). I have no doubt that I would have went through with my plans, if it hadn't been for reading your words of advice and encouragement. I told myself that if someone as incredible as Anna has been through the kind of inner hell that I've lived with, and figured out a way to climb out of that hole, then maybe there is a different option other than the permanent solution that I had been planning. I've pretty much been an agnostic on the question of whether there is a God or not, and if he actually intervenes in a person's life, but your letter came at the absolute lowest point in my life. You could have easily blown off writing me back, especially after the unfriendly way I treated you when we worked together, but you didn't. If the situation had been reversed, I've wondered if I would have made the effort to write you back. I guess that just shows the kind of character you possess. Since then I've been doing a lot of reading about depression and ways to fight it. Between that and giving up weed, I am actually having days where I feel alive again. That's something I haven't felt in many, many years. I know that decades of seeing the world in a negative light won't be changed overnight, and I still may have bad days, but with examples like yourself, and hard work on my part, I have a chance at having a better life. However my life ends up, it is completely up to me whether I make the changes to help myself or not.

Lastly Anna, and it wouldn't surprise me if many people have told you this, there is something special about you. Along with your other traits, (super intelligent, beautiful, extremely hard working, friendly, thoughtful towards others, reliable, self-confident, too many more to list), it is your charisma that really stands out. You're the kind of person that can use your ability to draw people to you, and actually touch their lives, and in doing so make the world a better place. That's pretty rare in this world. I'm sure you will go on to do many great things in your life, maybe even helping other people like you've helped me.

It all started with your letter.

Thanks for everything you've done for me.

I chose to share this letter with you at the very beginning, to help illustrate why I decided to write this book. I know you are probably wondering why I feel that I can help you. The simple answer to that question is, because you are the old me, and if you choose, I can be the future you. I battled depression for years and came out of it not only as a survivor, but what I like to call a thriver. A thriver to me is someone who comes out of a horrible situation and embraces life beyond the average person. I believe, people like you and I, feel more deeply than the average person. We are able to feel pain deeper than the person next to us, but we are also able to feel happiness to the extreme as well. Some people have sensitive noses and can pick up a smell others cannot. Other people are more sensitive to touch and feel physical pain more easily. But you and I are more sensitive to emotions and feelings. Unlike the person who has an extreme sense of smell or the person who is more sensitive to touch – you and I can control our sensitivity with the proper knowledge and practice.

I have been where you are. All of our experiences may vary slightly, but I've been curled up in a ball on my bed. The pain seeping out of my eyes in the form of tears, as I counted the sleeping pills lying on the bed beside me. There were over two-hundred little blue pills laying there, a bottle of water, and a girl living in a dark world. I had the strength to talk myself out of attempting suicide multiple times throughout my depression, not because I didn't want to die, but rather because I was afraid of failing. I couldn't imagine having to live with a failed suicide attempt and I just wasn't certain those sleeping pills, or the razor blade, or crashing my car would do the trick. I just didn't trust myself enough to get the job done. And thank God for that, because I am so thankful that I'm alive today!

I battled depression for what felt like an eternity, but I beat it and have been depression free for over 6 years. I have the knowledge that I hope and feel will help you and many others beat depression. A lot of people who are depressed are still fighting with depression because they simply haven't discovered the way out.

I struggled with how to introduce this "cure" for depression. I don't want to call it a secret, because I don't think people are hiding it. I believe that:

1) People who have never had depression don't truly understand it.

2) Most people who have had depression are sadly still battling it.

3) Those who have beaten it, either don't understand how they did it or they just haven't spoken up.

Either way, I believe that ending your depression is as easy as changing a habit. But you lack the knowledge to do so simply because no one has ever taught you. My goal is to give you that knowledge so that you can use it to beat <u>your</u> depression.

And guess what? I did it and that's why I know you can do it too!

Chapter 2

I am going to keep this chapter as short as possible because I know you got this book hoping to get straight to the part that tells you how to end your depression. I do, however believe that before you can apply the solution to end your depression, you need to understand how depression has developed in you. The easiest way to illustrate how depression develops is by describing it as an avalanche. An avalanche begins with one little snowflake. After that snowflake, comes another one and another one, until eventually there is a pile of snow. The pile of snow continues to build turning into a huge heap of snow. Eventually, all you can see, smell, and touch is snow until one day the snow builds up so much that it has no choice but to give into gravity and come crashing down the mountain.

Just like an avalanche, depression begins with one little snowflake. Only in this case that snowflake is a negative thought. Eventually as negative thought after negative thought consumes your mind, you completely forget that underneath the snow is grass and seeds of beautiful flowers. Everywhere you look, all you can see is negativity. And just like the avalanche, you eventually give in to the negativity until it comes crashing down and takes over your life.

But guess what? At one point in your life, <u>you were happy</u>. I don't know how long ago that was, maybe a year ago or five years ago or even twenty years ago. How long it's been doesn't matter, it just matters that you were! The fact that you were happy once before, is proof that you can be happy again.

You probably don't remember the day your negativity began. It could have started with a thought as simple as, "I look fat" or "I'm not good enough" or "I should be married by now". Then the next day you had two negative thoughts. Six months later half of your thoughts in a day were negative. A year later, you were lucky if you had one positive thought a day. But guess what? You had a choice of whether to think negative thoughts or positive thoughts, and you chose negativity. The most important thing for you to understand right now, in this very moment, is that **depression is a choice**.

Am I saying that you chose to be unhappy? No, not at all. It was an unconscious decision that was made without realizing the effects it would have. I am however saying that if you continue to be unhappy, it is because you aren't choosing to be happy.

So then, am I saying that genetics have nothing to do with depression? No, I'm not. I most definitely believe that genetics influence our probability of having depression. Depression runs in my family. But, I am saying no matter how strong your genetics are; you're stronger!

Am I saying circumstances or your environment can't be influencing your depression? No. Part of my depression was a result of my past. But, just like me, I know you can control how that circumstance makes you feel.

You didn't just wake up one morning and were all of a sudden depressed. There were signs that it was coming. You had no idea how to recognize those signs though, because you didn't even know what depression was before it took over your life. The good news is I'm not going to just teach you how to go into remission from depression. I'm going to teach you how to cure yourself of depression and prevent it from happening again!

Chapter 3

See, I told you I would keep that as short as possible! And on a happy note, you made it through to this point without killing yourself – congratulations! Ha ha?

Alright, alright! Perhaps I could have picked a better joke for the audience, BUT let me remind you, you are choosing whether to enjoy the joke or hate me for it. In this case, enjoying it would be the positive thought and hating me would definitely be negative. Choose the positive response!

So this is the chapter where I tell you how you are going to change your life. I hope you're as excited as I am, because honestly, if I help even just one person with this book, then it was well worth it.

I need you to start this chapter in a quiet room, by yourself. If you are reading this while you are out and about, at the doctor's office, or sitting at your desk at work, please put it on hold and continue at home. This part is very important and I need your full, undivided attention, in a place where you feel comfortable and are able to be undisturbed.

Ok, are you in a quiet room? Good! I am about to do something that's going to come off as a little hokey, but hopefully when I explain later you will understand the purpose.

To start off, I want you to sit down somewhere comfortable and take a good 10 seconds to just shake out your body parts, loosen up, take a deep breath, and relax. I want you to start off by breathing in really deep and then letting it out. Do that a couple times, and then return to the book.

Now, I want you to close your eyes and tell yourself where you feel the pain in your body. Tell yourself where the depression hurts. Don't just point out one spot that hurts, I want you to sit with the pain you feel, take an inventory of your body and the pain inside, and tell yourself everywhere you hurt. It's ok to let all of your emotions out as you feel the pain. Close your eyes and take the time to do this now.

Next, I want you to think of something that you enjoy. It can be anything, your child, a sport, eating ice cream. I don't care what it is, but there is something out there that you enjoy. Now, close your eyes and imagine yourself doing this thing that you enjoy.

What do you feel inside of you? Do you feel happiness? Do you feel power?

What positive feeling does imagining yourself doing this thing, bring to you?

Continue to breathe slowly and close your eyes and answer these questions to yourself.

Now that you've identified this feeling, I want you to close your eyes and tell yourself where in your body you feel this good feeling? Sit there and just let yourself feel it for a minute, and find where in your body that feeling resides.

Ok, now imagine that feeling in your chest or your arm or your face, wherever it was that you felt it, imagine it is a ball of energy. Close your eyes and imagine yourself doing whatever it is that you enjoy again, and feel that ball of positive energy in that body part again.

With your eyes closed, slowly expand that positive energy through the limb closest to it. Feel it slowly spreading through that limb. Then slowly spread it to the next limb and the next, until you have spread it through your arms, your fingers, your chest, your head, your shoulders, your thighs and calves, feet and toes.

Once you have spread the positive energy through your entire body, I want you to just sit there with your eyes closed and feel that good feeling through your entire body. Sit for as long as you want, feeling the goodness through your body and only return to the book when you are ready. There is no rush.

How do you feel? I told you it would feel a little hokey, but hopefully you were able to feel relieved for even just a moment from the pain you have been feeling

The exercise that I just shared with you is what saved my life. It's what opened my mind and hopefully what will open your mind to what I'm going to teach you. Don't worry, this exercise is not my answer to your depression, it is simply an illustration to prove a point that I'm going to share with you.

Perhaps your experience has been similar to mine. I went to multiple doctors throughout my battle with depression to get refills on my anti-depressants over the years. Not a single one of those doctors ever said anything to me other than, "Yep, you are clinically depressed, here is your prescription." Not a single doctor throughout those years said to me, "Sure, I will give you some pills, but first let's talk about why you feel this way." That is, until one doctor finally did and he saved my life. He saved me by speaking those seventeen words, followed by the exercise I just shared with you. He had me sit down in a chair and helped me feel better, for a moment in time. I'm not going to lie; I was embarrassed and self conscious. I hated every second of it until I felt the warmth of the good feeling spread through my body and my life changed right then and there. I didn't realize until years later the effect this exercise had on me, but I never did take the pills he prescribed for me, and I beat depression after that day.

Maybe you felt the awesome feeling from doing that exercise, the same as I did. Or maybe you didn't. That's ok too. But if you didn't get that same feeling, you need to understand that I was able to take the tiniest bit of a good feeling and transfer that feeling throughout my entire body and temporarily relieve the pain I had from my depression. How did I do that? WITH MY MIND!

If you have learned nothing up until this point from reading this book, remember the following, which will become your new mantra in life.

> The mind is a powerful thing!

That's the "secret", the "cure", or whatever you want to call it. This is the foundation you will build your freedom from depression on.

Sure, I'm going to give you a lot more knowledge here, but at the end of the day it all boils down to this. Plain and simple, the mind is a powerful thing. It is much more powerful than you can ever imagine. It is your weapon to beat depression. I don't care if you have the gene that says you will be clinically depressed forever, because your mind is way more powerful than that gene! I don't care if you had the worst childhood imaginable and emotions you don't understand consume you as a result, because your mind is way more powerful than any emotion! I don't care what your reason is for your depression, because your MIND IS WAY MORE POWERFUL than any reason!

So, here are the four simple steps that you are going to use to win this battle.

Step 1: You are going to make a conscious choice right now to be happy.

Step 2: You are going to recognize how strong your mind is and choose to put yourself in control.

Step 3: You are going to change a habit… just one habit.

Step 4: You're going to be happy

Those seem easy enough, right? Good, because they are! Let me go into more detail on each of them.

Step 1: Make the conscious choice right now to be happy

This seems kind of obvious I know, but depression clouds your decision making skills. It confuses you. It makes you forget that you even have the option. So right here, right now, make the conscious choice to be happy. Say it out loud.

I CHOOSE TO BE HAPPY!

And don't stop saying it, every single day. Put a reminder in your phone that goes off right before work that says, "I choose to be happy!" Write it on your mirror. Get a tattoo for all I care. Whatever you do, remind yourself of this choice, but you can NEVER forget it. The only way you can be happy is if you choose to be!

Step 2: Recognize how strong your mind is and choose to put yourself in control

Your depression has beaten you down and stolen your confidence in yourself. Tell your depression to go suck an egg (not what I'd like to say right now, but I'm trying to be classy here). It's time to take back the control of your own life. Realize how strong your mind is and remind yourself that YOU are in control of your life and what happens in it.

Step 3: Change the habit

All of the steps I've mentioned are extremely important, but this right here is the KEY, the bread and butter, to beating your depression. This step takes practice and it takes a bit of work, but once you master it, you will be a changed person and SO happy!

It's imperative that you understand that thoughts create emotions. Whatever you think, will result in the emotions you feel. People act based on emotions, so the emotions you feel from the thoughts you create, will result in the actions you take and the results you get.

So here is what you have to do. I talked earlier about how depression creeps in and takes over. I illustrated this with the avalanche analogy. One day you had a negative thought, and then another, and another, until eventually negativity took over your life. This is the end of your negative thoughts. From now on, this is what you are going to practice every single day of your life until it becomes second nature, and it will, I promise.

RECOGNIZE IT

Anytime a negative thought enters your brain, recognize it. Point it out and say, "Hey, that's a negative thought, that doesn't belong here!"

STOP IT

Don't let the thought go any further. Once you recognize it, put on the brakes, and stop it. Picture yourself jumping in front of the thought, with your left arm on your hip, and your right hand extended out, and the words flowing from your mouth, "STOP... in the name of love..." That's seriously what I do. It helps to physically imagine you stopping the thought. Choose your own image that is applicable to you (especially for you guys out there) and watch yourself stopping the thought every single time.

CHANGE IT

Figure out how you can make that negative thought positive and then do it. I'm not saying you can't understand that there is a bad situation that happened or that you have to be one of those fake bubbly people that just run around acting happy all the time. The difference between them and you is that you are going to really truly be happy. It's ok to recognize that something is not ideal. Accept that, be bummed about it even, BUT don't let negative thoughts consume you. Catch the negative thought, and make it positive.

> For example: You just found out a co-worker got a promotion that you had wanted. Some thoughts you might have are, "That jerk stole MY promotion!" or "I shouldn't have said that one thing and then I would have gotten it. I'm so stupid!" These thoughts are not

healthy. A positive thought would be, "Well, I'm bummed I didn't get the promotion, but good for 'so-and-so', they deserve it. I will just have to put in some extra work and prove that they need me the next time around!" So now, rather than sitting there gritting your teeth at work and stewing over something you honestly can't even change, you have chosen to be happy for the person who got the promotion and chose a constructive way to deal with the rejection. You will work even harder and prove yourself next time around. And now you have a goal to work towards as well.

In Summary

1) Choose to be happy
2) Recognize how strong your mind is and choose to put yourself in control
3) Change the habit – remember you create the thoughts that result in your emotions
    a. Recognize the thought
    b. Stop the thought
    c. Change the thought

These are the steps you are going to take to bring positivity back into your life. Like I said, it takes practice. You didn't change that habit of biting your nails overnight did you? No. You bit it, then you thought, "Dang it, I'm not supposed to be doing that." And you remembered it for an hour and then you bit your nail again. And you reprimanded yourself again and finally got to a point where you could get through a day without an incident, then a week, and a month. Then before you knew it, you created a new habit of not biting your nails. Just like when you finally stopped biting your nails, they started growing longer each day; as you start changing your thoughts, you are going to grow happier every day.

Which leads us to…

Step 4: You're going to be happy

This means exactly what it says, YOU ARE GOING TO BE HAPPY! If you have problems that need fixed in your life, you're going to be able to start thinking through them rationally and dealing with them properly. AND not only are you going to be happy now, you are going to continue to be happy. Why? Because by understanding how depression takes hold of your life and how you fixed it, you are going to recognize when your thoughts start turning negative and you're going to kick into battle mode and fight those thoughts before they ever even affect your happiness again.

I'm going to congratulate you now, because I KNOW that you're going to be successful with this. Follow these steps and then come back in a month and tell me how you feel. Will you be 100% in a month, probably not, but I guarantee you will be feeling much better and able to see the beauty in the world again. It is only a matter of time before you can look back and say, "I beat depression!"

So this chapter was the meat and potatoes of beating your depression. But, we can't survive off meat and potatoes alone, right? We need vegetables and even desert at times to keep us sane. So the next chapter is just that – the extra sides that are going to take you to the next level of happiness.

Chapter 4

Although beating depression is the main goal, most people want to achieve the greatest happiness possible in their life. I can honestly say that I have achieved a level of happiness that many people will never experience because I have taken supplemental steps to be EVEN happier. People, who have been truly clinically depressed, tend to have other issues aside from the avalanche effect of negativity. Once they reverse the tendency of thinking negative, that is a great time to start focusing on other ways to increase their happiness. The more ways you can increase your happiness, the more power you have against depression when it comes knocking on your door again – which it will. Taking extra steps to increase your happiness, is like giving yourself that many more weapons to draw when you start feeling low.

Therapy

Although depression ran in my family and genetically I had a higher possibility of becoming a victim to it, I do believe that there were things from my childhood that influenced depression actually taking a hold of me. One of the best things I've ever done for myself was go to therapy.

Choosing a therapist can be hard and you may not find the right one the first time or even the second time around. I went through multiple therapists before I found the perfect one for me. Once I found him, he knew how to help me and it felt amazing to finally get answers to why I turned out to be who I am today. Half of the battle to finding long lasting happiness is learning and understanding what makes you tick and what triggers your demons. I discovered reasons I reacted to situations the way I did. I discovered how to recognize feelings that I had, that weren't even associated with what I was reacting to, but was really associated to things from my past. Numerous relationships had failed in my life because of reactions I was having to things that had already passed in my life.

My discoveries during therapy may be completely different than yours. Maybe therapy isn't even something you need, but I highly recommend therapy to everyone, if for no other reason than just to have a deeper understanding of who you are. The more you know about yourself, the stronger you become as a person.

There are other forms of therapy as well, rather than going to see a therapist. Some people choose to write out their thoughts and are able to create their own therapy. Everyone learns about themselves in different ways. I recommend finding yourself through whatever therapy leads to the most self discovery.

Medicine

Let me clarify what I mean when I say medicine. First off, I don't think that taking medicine to cover the problem is ever a fix. I do however feel that some people have imbalances that need to be addressed through medicines or supplements. I personally take natural supplements daily that are recommended for people who suffer from depression. I don't take the supplements because I am depressed; I take them because I have a tendency to be naturally moodier than most people. I have a hard time managing my moodiness without having the supplements to help balance me out. They give me more energy, keep me more rational, and just give me a little extra "pep in my step" so-to-speak.

Natural supplements are not the only way to achieve balance for people and may not be for everyone. Sometimes people function better by taking a small dose of antidepressants or anxiety medicine. If a prescription gives someone the balance they need to be more stable and it isn't used to just mask the problem, then it can be a great supplement for those who are more prone to depression.

Simple Exercises

This "supplement" can honestly be whatever you find that makes you happy. By simple exercises, I am referring to little things that increase your overall mood and positivity. For example, laughing more often. I dated a guy once who indirectly taught me the importance of lightening the mood when I was upset or bothered by something. Anytime I would feel unhappy emotions, he would do something to make me laugh and as soon as I cracked a smile or giggled, everything felt less serious. I felt a million times better just because of that one moment of happiness. Now whenever I get upset, I try to find something that makes me laugh and it helps me put away the negativity and see the issue in a positive light.

Another example of a simple exercise to add happiness to your life is to make a list of things you are grateful for. I don't care how bad things get in life; everyone has something to be grateful for. Whether it's your children, the roof over your head, the food in your belly, or one person who goes out of their way to take care of you. No matter what life throws at us, there is no way we don't have anything to be grateful for. If you ever find yourself doubting this truth, think about those that are less fortunate than you. I guarantee you can find at least one thing to write down.

This leads me to the next exercise which is simply just to be kind to someone. Make a point to compliment someone each day or do a kind gesture. It can be for someone you know or a stranger. Doing nice things for other people adds positivity to our lives and it is true that we reap what we sow.

Another great way to increase your happiness is to learn something. People are happier when they feel good about themselves and who doesn't like being knowledgeable? This ties in a little with another important part of being happy, which is to have a hobby. By having a hobby, I mean having something that YOU love to do. Usually hobbies are something we are good at and passionate about. If you don't have a hobby, maybe you will stumble across something while you are out "learning". Hobbies are a great way to have a sense of self, something to remind you of who YOU are. Being that people tend to be passionate about things they are good at it, you will most likely be good at your hobby, which is also a great self esteem boost. It also opens doors to be more social, meet new people, and have things to add to discussions. All of these examples of simple exercises add positivity and happiness to your life. There are a million more things you can do to add to your happiness aside from these examples. Get creative!

Now comes the time where mama bird pushes baby bird out of the nest and watches the little bird fly. I have officially given you the knowledge you need to get out there and get back to life. You are on the road to being cured of your depression. You have been given the gift of a beautiful new life. Find what makes you happy, embrace it, and never forget that your mind is a powerful thing. You only get one life, now it's time to get it back and start living again!

Insert Metaphorical Push out of a Tree Here

www.ingramcontent.com/pod-product-compliance
Lightning Source LLC
Chambersburg PA
CBHW061315040426
42444CB00010B/2646